Amazing
Crocodiles
& Reptiles

WRITTEN BY
MARY LING

PHOTOGRAPHED BY
JERRY YOUNG

Dorling Kindersley · London

S

Illustrations by
Animals supplied by
Editorial consultan

Fir

9

Copyright
Cop

All rights reser
stored in a ret
means, electroni
without the

A CIP catalogue record for

ISBN 0-86318-546-0

Amazing
Crocodiles &
Reptiles

Colour reproduction by Colourscan, Singapore
Typeset by Windsorgraphics, Ringwood, Hampshire
Printed in Italy by A. Mondadori Editore, Verona

Contents

What is a reptile?

Reptiles are the last living relatives of the dinosaurs. For one hundred million years, reptiles were masters of the earth.

Family tree
What do snakes, lizards, crocodilians (that's crocodiles, alligators, gharials, and caimans) the turtle family, and the tuatara have in common? They're all reptiles, that's what.

Heat up, cool down
Reptiles are cold-blooded, which means they are the same temperature as the air or water around them. When they're cold, they bask in the sun, and when they get too hot, they pick a shady spot to cool down in.

Most reptiles swing their backs from side to side when they walk

Like most reptiles, crocodiles have short legs

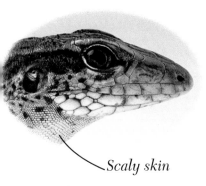

Scaly skin

No sweat
Basking in the sun all day would make you hot and sticky – and very thirsty. But reptiles have scaly, watertight skin from head to toe, so their bodies don't dry out.

Egg layers
Nearly all reptiles lay eggs. Most babies hatch out when they're ready, but the Nile crocodile gently cracks the eggs open with her teeth if she thinks they're taking too long.

New skin for old
All reptiles shed their skin. Some snakes shuffle out of theirs in one go. But lizards lose their skin bit by bit. Sometimes they even tug off the stubborn pieces with their teeth!

Scaly, dry skin has no hairs

Nifty movers
This dwarf crocodile lives in the forests of West Africa. It might look clumsy when it's walking, but it's quite a nifty mover once it's spied a tasty frog or fish!

Crocodiles lift their bodies off the ground when they walk

The incredible hunter

With powerful jaws studded with teeth and skin like a suit of armour, the Nile crocodile can overpower almost any animal it chooses.

Death roll
Crocodiles lunge out of the water as quick as a flash and clamp their victims with power-packed jaws. They spin and twist in the water to tear off bite-sized chunks of meat. Then they swallow the pieces of meat – whole.

Crocodiles only have about 50 meals a year

Fish eaters
Gharials have long, slim jaws with a hundred razor-sharp teeth. A quick sideways sweep of the head through the water traps a passing fish. Then, with one toss of the head, it's down the hatch.

Scales on tail form a spiky ridge

Crocodiles can't poke their tongues out

Sun seekers
Nile crocodiles can be found basking on river-banks all over tropical Africa. At 1.2 metres long, this croc still has a long way to go before it catches up with the longest Nile crocodile ever found – which measured 5.94 metres!

Man-made meal

For some crocodiles, humans are on the menu. So take care when you step on a floating log. It may be a lurking croc waiting to snap you up.

Diners' club

Crocodiles are not greedy. As many as 30 or 40 may join in a zebra feast, helping one another tear off morsels.

The crocodile god

The ancient Egyptians feared and worshipped Nile crocodiles so much that their god of power, Sobek, had a crocodile's head.

Living toothpick

When they get too hot, crocodiles rest with their mouths gaping open. They don't seem to mind when the plover bird picks leftover food from between their teeth.

11

Living in a box

The tortoise is a moving fortress. It has such a heavy shell to carry around that it can't run, jump, or swim. That's why it lives only on land.

Safe as houses
A tortoise's shell protects its whole body. The shell is made of bone and covered with a layer of tough scales made from the same stuff as your fingernails. The part that covers its back is joined to the tortoise's spine and ribs.

Little and large
There are about 40 different kinds of tortoise. Some are only a few centimetres long, but others measure well over a metre.

Home and away
When danger threatens, most tortoises and turtles pull their head and legs into their shells. But some, like this snake-necked turtle, just wind their long necks round and tuck their heads in.

Land   *Sea*   *Fresh water*

Feet apart

Plodding land tortoises have elephant-like feet. Sea turtles have front flippers like paddles. And turtles and terrapins which live in fresh and salty water, have webbed feet.

No teeth!

Tortoises and turtles do not have teeth. Instead, their jaws have razor-sharp edges that can snip twigs and tear flesh.

Groovy shells

Tortoises from the Galapagos Islands have tailor-made shells. On lush green islands, the tortoises have gently curving shells that don't get in the way when they're eating. But on islands where food is high up a branch, their shells have grooves behind the neck for easier high-rise eating.

Red-legged tortoise

This tortoise roams around in the humid forests of South America. At full size, its shell can be as long as 50 cm – that's quite a handful!

13

Slithering snakes

Snakes manage very well without legs. Some climb trees, some slither about on the ground, and others are expert swimmers. A few clever snakes can even glide through the air.

Snakes move from branch to branch by stretching out, head first

Markings look like piano keys

Deadly fangs

Some snakes are poisonous. When they fancy a bite to eat, they sink their sharp fangs into their victim and pump in a deadly poison. Then the feast begins.

Snake specs

Snakes have no eyelids. Instead, they have see-through scales covering their eyes like spectacles. When a snake sheds its skin, it gets new specs too.

Hundred flower rat snake

This snake can be found slinking along branches in the bamboo forests of southern China. One of its favourite meals is – you guessed it – rats!

Born swimmers

The yellow-bellied sea snake spends all its life in the water. It uses its flat tail like a paddle to zoom around at top speed.

Magnificent movers

Some snakes move in special ways. The sidewinder tiptoes across the American desert in a zigzag dance, keeping its belly off the hot sand.

Supper sense

Many snakes and lizards don't smell with their noses like we do. They flick their tongues in and out to "taste" the air for a passing meal. Then the scent is sent down the line to a special smelling organ in the mouth.

Big mouth

Having a snake's jaws would make mealtimes a lot more simple. A snake can open its jaws so wide that it can swallow a meal much bigger than its head – whole.

Amazing alligators

Next time you come across a crocodilian with its mouth closed, check its teeth. If the fourth tooth on the bottom pokes out, then it's a crocodile. But if all its bottom teeth are tucked in, then it's an alligator, like this one.

Caiman

Watch out for snouts
A snout is a crocodilian's greatest weapon. Gharials have long, narrow jaws for catching fish. Alligators have broad, stout snouts. Crocodiles and caimans have slimmer, medium-sized jaws.

Alligator

Crocodile

Gharial

An alligator can grow forty or fifty new sets of teeth in a lifetime

Smash
Alligators and crocodiles can't chew food before they swallow it, because their teeth are only for grabbing and tearing. So they swallow stones to help smash up the food they've eaten.

Belly full
Stones also help to stop them bobbing up and giving the game away when they're stalking prey in the water.

What a racket!
A big alligator's bellow is quite something to hear. It sounds like a huge, noisy engine. And once one alligator gets going, its neighbours soon join in.

Record breaker
You'd have trouble getting the longest American alligator ever found into your bedroom *and* closing the door behind you. It was 5.84 m long.

American alligator
Next time you're in the swamps of Florida, look out for this alligator. If it's resting with its mouth wide open, don't worry – it's just feeling hot and trying to cool down.

Strange shapes and shells

Tall, strong shells make safe homes on land. In the water, light slim shells work best. But wherever turtles live, they have ways of staying extra safe.

Leather shell

The leatherback is the largest sea turtle around. It can weigh as much as 916 kg. Instead of a heavy shell and scales, it has tiny bony plates under its leathery skin.

Fold-away neck

This snake-necked turtle lives in rivers in Australia. It hunts fish, snails, and shrimps among rocks with the help of its hosepipe neck, which is as long as its body.

The snake-necked turtle tucks its neck sideways around its shell

Prickly turtle?

When it's born, the spiny forest turtle's shell is very soft. The shell's jagged edge gives the young turtle extra protection while it waits for its armour to toughen up.

Stinkpots

These little turtles live in North America. When birds try to pick them up, the turtles let off a disgusting smell. That's why they're called stinkpots.

Crunch proof

Sharing the river with alligators must be nerve-racking. So the Florida red-bellied turtle has a strong, high shell to protect itself from the alligators' deadly crunching jaws.

Flat as a ...

This is one pancake you won't want to eat. The African pancake tortoise has a flat shell. When danger threatens, it can run quite fast (for a tortoise) and squeeze into tiny spaces where enemies can't reach.

Webbed feet, just right for fast river swimming

Snorkelling turtle

The matamata turtle of Brazil sits on the river-bed waiting for supper to swim by. Using its long, stretchy neck, it pokes its nostrils out of the water to take a breath, without having to move and frighten the fish.

Useful lizard

Lizards live in every part of the world, except in deepest, coldest Antarctica. Some of them make wonderful house guests – they run around lapping up flies and mosquitoes.

Ancient tuatara
It may look like a lizard but, in the family of reptiles, the tuatara is in a group on its own. In the time of the dinosaurs, its relatives lived all over the world. Now, they live only in parts of New Zealand.

Early riser
Most geckos prefer the night life, but the Madagascar day gecko wakes up in the day. It hangs about in trees in the forests of Madagascar, eating small insects and fruit. For a special treat, it likes a lick of honey.

Geckos lick their eyeballs to keep them clean

Prickly lizard
When it senses danger, the armadillo lizard just rolls up into a hoop, tucks its tail in its mouth, and sits tight. Its tough, prickly spikes help to shield its belly, the only soft part of its body.

Shattered

The Pallas's glass snake is a lizard with no legs. What's more, it has a special "snap off" tail. If it's caught, its tail breaks up into tiny wriggling pieces, while the rest of it makes a quick getaway.

Don't step on my tail

The Oriental long-tailed lizard has a clever way of getting around. It throws itself from stalk to stalk in its grassy meadow home, keeping balance with its amazingly long tail.

Lash out

When the Gould's monitor lizard is threatened, it hisses loudly and rears up on its back legs to frighten its attacker.

Skin changes

Chameleons change colour to suit how hot or sunny it is. This chameleon has a leafy pattern on its skin from sunbathing on a leafy branch. The part of its skin that was in the shade hasn't changed colour.

21

Slow movers

Imagine carrying your home around on your back. You wouldn't win many races.

Head for danger

The big-headed turtle can't tuck its head into its shell when it's in danger – it doesn't fit. But its long tail helps it clamber over rocks and plants for a quick getaway.

Many happy returns

One advantage of taking life slowly is that you can live to a ripe old age. One male Marion's tortoise lived to be 152! That's a lot of candles on a birthday cake.

Powerful paddles

Sea turtles look exhausted crawling on land, but they glide gracefully in water. They can speed along at up to 70 km/h if need be, flapping their powerful flippers like wings.

Thick shell under belly protects against rough stones and twigs

The hare and the tortoise
In an old story, a hare and a tortoise had a race. The hare got so far ahead that he took a nap. When he woke up, he was too late. The tortoise had plodded steadily all the way and won the race!

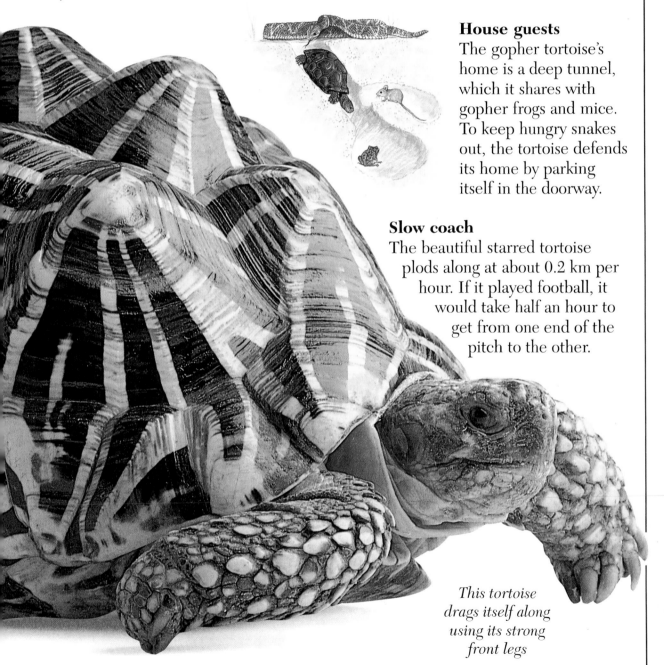

House guests
The gopher tortoise's home is a deep tunnel, which it shares with gopher frogs and mice. To keep hungry snakes out, the tortoise defends its home by parking itself in the doorway.

Slow coach
The beautiful starred tortoise plods along at about 0.2 km per hour. If it played football, it would take half an hour to get from one end of the pitch to the other.

This tortoise drags itself along using its strong front legs

23

Crocodiles in water

Crocodiles live at the water's edge where they enjoy the best of both worlds: land and water. On land, they move clumsily. But in the water, they are elegant, powerful swimmers.

See through
When we dive underwater, we have to wear goggles to protect our eyes. Crocs have three eyelids – two where eyelids normally are and a third, see-through lid which pulls across from side to side for safe underwater sight.

The first croc?
An old Aboriginal story tells of a poor man called Ginja who caught on fire. He rushed into the river to put the fire out. But the heat had blistered his skin. Ginja became the first crocodile.

Caimans can hold their breath underwater

Diving equipment
Catching and swallowing prey underwater could be tricky if crocodiles gulped too much water. A muscular flap which closes off the mouth from the breathing tubes stops them choking.

Muscular flap

Modern caiman
The spectacled caimans of South America have learnt to live in a modern world. They have discovered that man-made dams and cattle ponds make comfortable homes.

A rug of mud
Mud makes a wonderful blanket – cools you if you're hot, warms you if you're feeling chilly. It also makes you a less inviting meal for annoying insects.

Crocodile tears
People used to think that crocodiles shed tears when they ate their victims. Now we know that they're just getting rid of all the salt they've swallowed in the water!

A strong tail
Crocs tuck their legs in and use their tails to push them through the water. Their tails are so strong and powerful that some crocodiles have been known to "tail-walk".

Eat or be eaten

Being a slow mover can be a problem if you don't fancy plants or snails and worms for dinner. Some turtles have clever ways of snaring meals that go whizzing by.

Vacuum eater

The matamata stands so still on the muddy river-bed that its lumpy shell looks like a rock. When fish swim near, it suddenly opens its enormous mouth. In rushes the water – and the fish, too.

Living larder
The first explorers in the Galapagos Islands found the tortoises there very useful. They trapped them and ate them on the long journey home. Until then the tortoises had had no enemies.

Turtle treats

Some baby turtles don't even get to taste their first meal. As newly hatched green turtles run down the beach towards the sea for their first swim, hungry sea-gulls swoop down and snatch up the unlucky ones.

Open wide

The alligator snapping turtle sits quietly on the river-bed with its mouth wide open, waiting for its next meal to swim by. On its tongue it has a bright pink growth that looks just like a worm wiggling about.

Crunch

When a curious fish comes too close, sharp hooked jaws slam shut on it.

Watch-dog turtles

Loggerhead turtles crush crabs and clams in their vicious jaws. Their bite is so savage that the Sri Lankans call them dog turtles.

Snapped up

If you ever come across a snapping turtle, keep your fingers well away. It will attack just about anything that comes too close to its powerful beak.

The snapping turtle's massive head and arms can't fit into its shell

Hatching out

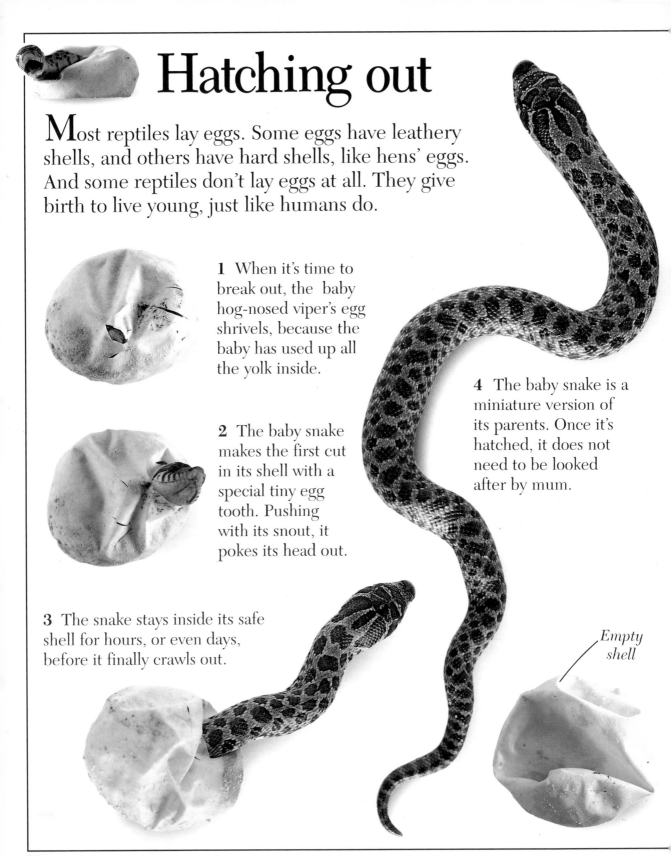

Most reptiles lay eggs. Some eggs have leathery shells, and others have hard shells, like hens' eggs. And some reptiles don't lay eggs at all. They give birth to live young, just like humans do.

1 When it's time to break out, the baby hog-nosed viper's egg shrivels, because the baby has used up all the yolk inside.

2 The baby snake makes the first cut in its shell with a special tiny egg tooth. Pushing with its snout, it pokes its head out.

4 The baby snake is a miniature version of its parents. Once it's hatched, it does not need to be looked after by mum.

3 The snake stays inside its safe shell for hours, or even days, before it finally crawls out.

Empty shell

Long wait

The estuarine crocodile makes a nest of rotting plants to keep its eggs warm. After the eggs are laid, the mother guards them until they hatch.

Caring parents

When baby crocodiles hatch, their mother gently gathers as many as she can into her mouth and places them in a nursery pool.

Egg snatchers

During the nesting season, reptile parents watch out for monitor lizards, whose favourite meal is a batch of fresh reptile eggs.

Alligator guard

The Florida red-bellied turtle lays her eggs in an alligator's nest. The reward for risking her life to do this is a safe, warm place to keep her eggs and a free egg minder.

So many eggs

This green turtle's mother travels a very long way to lay her eggs on the same beach every year. And of the 2,000 eggs she lays in her lifetime, only three will become adults.